395

Published by
*Federation of Family
History Societies
(Publications) Ltd.*
The Benson Room
Birmingham and
Midland Institute,
Margaret Street,
Birmingham B3 3BS
United Kingdom

Copyright © Audrey Collins

ISBN 1-86006-051-X

First published 1997

Basic facts about . . .

Using the Family Records Centre

Audrey Collins

SERIES EDITOR
Pauline M. Litton

FEDERATION OF FAMILY HISTORY SOCIETIES

D1269990

Printed and bound by
Oxuniprint,
Great Clarendon Street,
Oxford OX2 6DP

CONTENTS

THE FAMILY RECORDS CENTRE

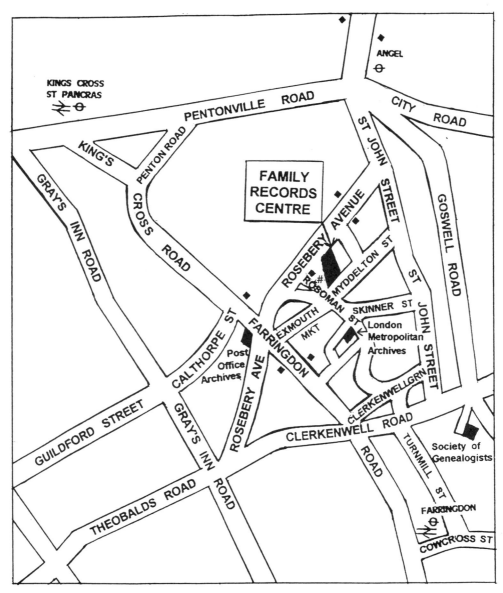

◆ Bus Stops   # Garnault Place (4 disabled parking bays)

INTRODUCTION

This is not a book on how to trace your family history. What it aims to do instead is to help you make the best use of the Family Records Centre. It assumes a basic knowledge of using the systems of Civil Registration, Census and Wills in England and Wales, and of the sort of information they contain. There are several good basic books on these subjects, which are listed in the bibliography.

The Family Records Centre combines the former holdings of the Office for National Statistics (ONS) at St Catherine's House with the census and some other records from the Public Record Office (PRO), which used to be at Chancery Lane. In addition, there are new resources, previously unavailable at either location. The Centre occupies three floors of a brand new block, with cloakroom and lunch-room facilities in the basement. Civil Registration indexes to births, marriages and deaths are on the ground floor, with Census and other former PRO material on the first floor. There are toilets on each floor, including those for the disabled, and access by lift to all floors. There is also a ramp from pavement level to the entrance. Baby-changing facilities are in the basement. Readers' tickets or proof of identity are not required. The Family Records Centre welcomes visits from Family History Societies and other groups, but needs to be notified in advance. Please arrange your visit by ringing 0181-392 5300.

The Family Records Centre

1 Myddelton Street, Islington, London EC1R 1UW
Certificate enquiries Phone 0151-471 4800 Minicom 0151-471 4530
ONS General enquiries Phone 0181-233 9233
PRO General enquiries Phone 0181-392 5300 Minicom 0181-392 5308
Fax 0181-392 5307
Internet: http://www.open.gov.uk/pro/prohome.htm

Opening hours:

Monday, Wednesday, Friday	9.00am - 5.00pm
Tuesday	10.00am - 7.00pm
Thursday	9.00am - 7.00pm
Saturday	9.30am - 5.00pm

Closed Sundays and Bank Holiday weekends including Saturdays (Late night and Saturday opening is for a trial period, to be reviewed late summer 1997).

GETTING THERE

The first test of your research skills is to find the Family Records Centre. At the time of writing, the Borough of Islington has not put up any signposts, so you will need to find the building with the aid of a map, or detailed directions.

Public Transport

The nearest Underground station is **Angel** (Northern Line), but **Farringdon** (Metropolitan, Circle, Hammersmith & City and Thameslink) is also within walking distance, as is **Kings Cross** (all the above lines, plus Victoria, Piccadilly and of course the rail terminus itself). In central London, the distance above ground between Underground stations is often quite short — the famous Underground map is really a diagram, and gives no idea of scale. It is often easier to use a station which is not the nearest to your destination if it is on a line which is more convenient from your starting point. For example, if you are using the Metropolitan, Circle or Hammersmith & City lines, it is better to alight at Farringdon and walk from there, than to change to the Northern line at Kings Cross to get to Angel, as the change involves escalators, steps, two sets of ticket barriers and a fair amount of walking. You may also be influenced by the means of access to particular stations. All Underground stations in central London have either stairs, escalators or lifts, or some combination of them. Angel is one of the deeper stations, with two escalators between platform and ground level. There are escalators and some steps from the Northern, Piccadilly and Victoria lines to ground level at Kings Cross; from the Circle, Metropolitan and Hammersmith & City lines there are two flights of steps up to ground level. Full details of access to all underground stations can be found in *Access to the Underground,* a guide produced by London Transport for disabled passengers. Their Unit for Disabled Passengers may be contacted on 0171-918 3312 for more information. Bus and underground maps can be obtained free of charge from London Underground headquarters, Tourist Information Centres and many Underground stations. For up-to-date information you can ring London Transport on 0171-222 1234, Minicom 0171-918 3015.

Buses which pass close to the Centre are 63, which runs from **Kings Cross** and down Farringdon Road, which is a short walk from Myddelton Street; buses 19, 38 and 171a all run along Rosebery Avenue, and therefore stop closest to the Family Records Centre. The 171a also goes to Waterloo, and stops in the Aldwych. The Aldwych is convenient for Somerset House and is easily reached from Charing Cross by bus or on foot. For anyone arriving in London at Victoria station, the 38 also runs from there. There are no mainline stations on the route of the 19 bus, but like the last two it stops outside Angel underground station, for anyone who prefers not to walk from there. Although the walk takes only about 10 minutes, it does involve crossing at a very busy junction.

Anyone arriving at **Liverpool Street,** or **Moorgate** can take the Circle, Metropolitan or Hammersmith & City Lines to Farringdon, and from **Paddington,** the Metropolitan or Hammersmith & City Lines. From **Fenchurch** Street the way to Farringdon is by the Circle Line from Tower Hill. **Cannon Street** and **Victoria** are also on the Circle Line, but this is not the quickest route from either of them. From **Cannon Street** the best route is to walk to Bank station, then take the Northern Line to Angel. From **Victoria** take the Victoria Line to Kings Cross, then the Northern Line (City Branch) to Angel. From **Charing Cross** the best Underground route is the Northern Line to Euston, then change to the Northern Line (City Branch) for Angel. If your train calls at **London Bridge** on its way to Charing Cross, it is better to alight there and take the Northern Line (City Branch) to Angel. Arriving at **Marylebone** the best route is to walk to Baker Street, which is very close by, then Circle, Metropolitan or Hammersmith & City Line to Farringdon. This is quicker than using the Bakerloo Line, which involves a long change at Baker Street. **Euston** is only two stops from Angel on the Northern Line (City Branch). These are not the only routes you can use, and you may find better ones for yourself, but this information should at least be of some help in finding your way to an unfamiliar location.

Car parking

There is very little on-street parking. If you bring a car, National Car Parks have sites on Farringdon Road and Skinner Street (Skinner Street is cheaper for long-stay parking). For disabled drivers, the Family Records Centre has a limited number of parking spaces, which must be booked in advance by ringing 0171-533 6400. There are also some single yellow lines in nearby streets where orange badge holders may be able to park, and 4 disabled parking bays in Garnault Place.

Eating and Drinking

The Family Records Centre provides a lunch room with tables and chairs, but the catering facilities consist only of vending machines for drinks and snacks. However, this is not a problem, as there are plenty of places to eat nearby. In particular, Exmouth Market, just opposite the Centre, has pubs, cafes and take-away food outlets. If the weather is good, there are gardens on either side of Rosoman Street, heading towards the London Metropolitan Archives (formerly Greater London Record Office) in Northampton Street, where you can picnic. Unfortunately for anyone on a coach party, most of the cafes have closed by around 5pm, so there is nowhere in the immediate vicinity, (apart from pubs) to buy an early evening meal or snack before boarding the coach for the journey home.

Other Facilities

The nearest banks to Myddelton Street are in the area around the Angel station, and there are several around Kings Cross. There is also a Link cash machine next to the Post Office Archives. There are no banks, building societies or cash dispensers on the route from Farringdon Station.

There are five card and coin payphones inside the Family Records Centre.

Other Record Offices

For anyone researching London or Middlesex ancestry (apart from the City of London and Westminster), the London Metropolitan Archives (formerly Greater London Record Office) are only a few minutes walk away. Only slightly further away are the Post Office Archives, at Mount Pleasant. The Society of Genealogists Library is also within walking distance.

CONTENTS OF THE FAMILY RECORDS CENTRE

Ground Floor (ONS)

The foyer contains the security desk, where all bags must be opened for inspection, and a bookshop selling PRO publications, maps and other family history books and magazines.

The new ONS search room is much more spacious than the old one at St Catherine's House, and is all on one level. The index volumes are on two shelves of the racking, not three as they used to be in some places. This means that it is generally easier than before to get close to the books you want to search, although it can still get very crowded in the most popular sections.

Indexes brought from St Catherine's House:

- ◆ Births, marriages & deaths in England & Wales from 1 July 1837
- ◆ Adoptions in England & Wales from 1927
- ◆Consular births, marriages & deaths 1849-1965
- ◆ UK High Commission births and deaths up to 1966
- ◆ Marine births & deaths 1837-1965
- ◆ Air births & deaths 1947-1965
- ◆ Regimental Registers of births 1761-1924
- ◆ Chaplains' returns of births & deaths 1796-1880
- ◆ Ionian Islands births, marriages & deaths 1818-1964
- ◆ Army returns of births 1881-1945
- ◆ Army returns of marriages 1881-1965
- ◆ Army returns of deaths 1881-1950
- ◆ Service Departments' returns of births 1956-1965
- ◆ Service Departments' returns of deaths 1951-1965
- ◆ Natal & South Africa deaths 1899-1902
- ◆ Indian Services War deaths 1914-1921, 1939-1945
- ◆ Army deaths 1914-1921, 1939-1948
- ◆ Naval deaths 1914-1921, 1939-1948
- ◆ RAF deaths 1939-1948
- ◆ Births, marriages & deaths abroad from 1966

Plus the following new facilities:

◆ Limited facilities for disabled users to consult the indexes on microfiche. These places must be booked in advance.
◆ Electoral registers for England and Wales for the last year before the current one.
◆ On-line computer link to New Register House for Scottish Civil Registration Indexes of births, marriages & deaths from 1855, Divorces from 1984, Old Parochial Registers 1553-1854 and index to the 1891 census for Scotland. Please note, this service is not available on Saturdays, and time on the computer terminals must be booked. A fee is payable, by cash or cheque only.

First Floor (PRO)

On entering the PRO reading room, you are given a pass which has the number of your microfilm reader on it. If you leave the first floor for any reason, you must hand this in, and obtain a new one if you return. Seats cannot be booked in advance. There are 235 microfilm readers, grouped in four areas, three of them (A, B & C) for the census. The fourth (W) is for Prerogative Court of Canterbury (PCC) Wills and Administrations up to January 1858 and the other records brought from Chancery Lane. In the census area, sections A and B are closest to the reference areas and film cabinets. Some readers have found that the room is too light to read the screens in comfort. If this is likely to be a problem for you, area C is better-shaded than the other two. Beside each reader is a black or white box with its number on it. Whenever you take a film out of the cabinets, this box should be put in its place. There are 6 reader-printers for film, distributed around the reading room, plus one for fiche, and a photocopier, all self-service. Payment is by cash or a re-chargeable card (which is cheaper if you want a lot of copies). Cards can be bought at the Reprographic Services Desk. The machines do not give change. The staff can also make copies from film for you, at a higher cost.

The actual records held are all on microfilm. The 1891 census was formerly also available on microfiche, but this has been withdrawn for a trial period.

The records held are:

◆ Census returns for England, Wales, Isle of Man & Channel Islands 1841-1891
◆ (PCC) Wills and Administrations 1358 — Jan 1858
◆ Estate Duty (often called Death Duty) registers 1796-1857
◆ Indexes to Estate Duty registers 1796-1903
◆ Nonconformist registers up to 1857, including Quakers
◆ Indexes to Non-statutory Miscellaneous Foreign Registers of births, marriages & deaths

For more details see Amanda Bevan and Andrea Duncan's *'Tracing Your Ancestors in the Public Record Office'.*

There is also a collection of finding aids on this floor, including the following:

◆ International Genealogical Index (IGI) for the British Isles; 1881 Census Index for England, Wales, Channel Islands & Isle of Man; some surname indexes for other census years, mostly 1851; directories; maps and gazetteers; PCC and other pre-1858 will indexes in print; some Nonconformist lists and indexes; some printed parish registers for London; part of Boyd's Marriage Index (Second Miscellaneous Series); a selection of genealogical reference books; the Current Guide to the PRO (but no class lists — these will eventually be available as an on-line link when the PRO indexes are computerized); FamilySearch on CD-Rom.

Some of these are on microfiche, for which there are 26 readers. If you need to use one of these, find a vacant microfiche reader, and use the dummy card beside it to put in place of the fiche you wish to consult.

WHAT TO BRING WITH YOU

Do your homework before you set out, and work out *exactly* what you are going to search for. For Civil Registration searches in particular, prepare your search sheets or notebook in advance. Spiral-bound books have the advantage that they lie flat. If you use loose sheets, attach them to a clipboard. You can buy specially printed search sheets, but squared paper is also useful for ticking off the quarters as you check them. You will see people searching without doing this. This is either because they are very experienced, or very silly. Unless you fall into one of these categories, always tick off the quarters as you go along. When it is very busy, you may not always be able to look at the books in order, so it is better to trust your notes than your memory, so that you know exactly which volumes you need to go back to. Always carry spare pens or pencils, as there are few things more frustrating than getting settled in a good space, handy for the books you want to look at, only to find that your pencil breaks or your pen runs out, and you have to abandon it to fetch another one. If you bring someone with you it is not a good idea to search together. Two people cannot look at a book better than one, and you will get twice as much done if you search separately.

Money

You can pay for certificates with cash, cheque (cheque card required), credit card or debit card (ie Switch or Delta), but not Travellers Cheques. You may also want change for the vending machines and for photocopies. You will also need a £1 coin for a locker: this is a deposit, which you get back when you have finished with the locker, so it does not actually cost you anything at all. It is not necessary to carry large amounts of luggage and coats around the search room with you. Quite apart from the very real danger that your belongings may be stolen, or at least trodden on, it is very inconsiderate to other searchers. Most of the lockers are small ones, but coats and lockable, rigid bags such as briefcases can be secured on the coat racks. As the building is air-conditioned, you will find that you are most comfortable wearing ordinary indoor clothes; this is another good reason for leaving coats in the cloakroom.

A summary of the information you already have

You never know what a search will turn up, so it is a good idea to be able to check on dates and places in your family tree. This can take the form of a copy of the family tree, or a notebook with vital details about each individual, or family group sheets. There are a number of these on the market, or you can make up your own. The main requirement is that it should be compact, so you can keep it with you. There have been sightings of searchers with huge folders of family information, and even card index boxes, but this is not a good idea.

Fashion hints for genealogists

Wear comfortable clothes and shoes. Ideally, wear something with pockets, for your locker key, spare pencils etc. If you don't have pockets, a bum-bag, known more politely as a belt-purse, is a good investment.

USING THE ONS SEARCH ROOM

Search Room etiquette

There are no reserved places in the ONS Public Search Room, so it is up to each searcher to make their own space. This is not quite the free-for-all that you might expect. Obviously you want to find a place at a lectern close to the volumes you need to search. This will not always be possible at busy times, especially in the most popular sections (roughly 1880-1910 in births, deaths and marriages). The marriage section in particular can be very crowded, as searches there often cover a longer span of years. Once you have found a space, if you put your notebook or clipboard there then it is 'yours'. There is an unwritten rule that you do not put your things on top of someone else's, and in general this works reasonably well. Naturally there will always be a small minority who feel they have an absolute right to barge in, regardless, but most people are fairly polite. Having found a space, you can then start searching. Try to maintain the spirit of goodwill and co-operation by not spreading out too much. It really is not necessary to take up a lot of lectern space with the volume you are looking at, an open folder of notes next to it, and your coat and picnic lunch on the other side. If you are doing a long search or listing, you will want to move along as you do so, to be as close as possible to the volumes you want. With luck someone nearby will be trying to move in the opposite direction, with whom you can offer to swap places.

The Family Records Centre aims to be a user-friendly place with as few rules and regulations as possible. One of those few rules is that you should only remove one book from the shelves at a time. There are several reasons for this, one of which is that each book is very large and takes up a lot of room. The books are very heavy, and carrying more than one of them at a time can be downright dangerous. Another reason is to prevent damage to the books themselves. When searching for a marriage you may find what you hope is an entry for one of the parties, and be tempted to take out another book at the same time to check for the other name. When it is crowded, people sometimes achieve this by simply putting the second book on top of the open pages of the first one. Bearing in mind that some of these volumes are over a century old, this is obviously not a good idea. If you believe you have found one half of your marriage, make a note of it, put the book back, and then check the other volume.

The volume you want is missing

It may be that a book has been replaced on completely the wrong shelf, or someone is using it for a very long time. If this is the case, make a note of it and try again later. Sometimes a book is out for a few days because it is being repaired. When this happens, a dummy volume is put in its place, so that you know not to waste time looking for it. If you think that an entry you want may be in one of these missing volumes, ask at the Customer Service Desk, who can have the duplicate index checked for you. This cannot be done instantly, so you will be asked to return to the counter later in the day to obtain the result.

Where is this Registration District?

Each entry in the indexes has a Registration District (RD), followed by a volume number and page. You may find an with an RD the name of which is unfamiliar to you, so you need to know where it is, to see if it is the one you want. There are maps on the walls of the Search Room which show RDs with volume numbers and locations, but you may not want to abandon your hard-won space in search of one. Ray Wiggins' *St Catherine's House Districts* is small enough to carry around with you, but this is no help if you are in mid-search without a copy. A third possibility is to look for another RD which you do recognize and which has the same volume number, which means it is nearby. Failing that, try asking the person next to you; the chances are that someone within earshot will know the answer, and few family historians can resist giving others the benefit of their knowledge. Pauline Saul's *The Family Historian's Enquire Within* has a list of volume numbers with the counties where they occur.

Other enquiries

The staff at the Customer Service Desk can also give you information about RDs, such as which district a particular parish was in. As there were boundary changes from time to time, this might not always be the same one throughout. They can also supply the current addresses for local Registrars and other record offices, as well as General Register Offices or their equivalents outside England and Wales. You can also obtain an application form here for a search in the 1901 census, which is still in the custody of the Registrar General. You need to be a direct descendant or next of kin, of the person you are seeking and give a specific address to be searched. Only ages and birthplaces will be provided. A fee is payable for this service.

Ordering certificates

If you have been successful in your searches, you will probably want to order one or more certificates. Remember that you need full birth certificates, not short ones. When you fill in the forms, you may be surprised to find that the birth certificate application asks you for a great deal of infomation, but you need only fill in the details from the index, unless you are ordering a birth certificate from 1946 or later. This is simply to prevent fraudulent applications. If you are ordering up to three certificates you may use the Express Till; for four or more there is a single queue for the other four tills. Your certificates will be ready for collection four working days after you order them, or will be posted on the third working day. There is no extra charge for postage, even to overseas addresses. Saturday does not count as a working day, so orders placed on a Tuesday will be ready the following Monday, or be posted on Friday. Saturday orders are processed with the following Monday's business, and will be ready for collection on Friday. On the late night openings, Tuesday and Thursday, the tills are closed at 5pm, re-opening at 5.30pm. Orders taken after this are treated as the following day's transactions. Remember to allow for Bank Holidays. The only exception to this is the 24-hour Priority Service, which currently costs more than three times the price of an ordinary application. You can also order certificates by post, from the Postal Applications Section at Southport, but this costs at least twice as much as applications in person, more if you do not have the exact reference. If you are unable to visit the Family Records Centre in person, you will probably find it is cheaper to use a record agent, many of whom advertise in *Family Tree Magazine,* or your local Family History Society may run a courier service.

Reference-checking

If you are not sure you have found the right entry, you may use the back of the application form to have the entry checked against a known piece of information, called a 'checking point', and the certificate will only be issued if it agrees. You should only use a checking point you are absolutely sure of, and which you know will appear on the certificate. The back of each application form suggests the checking points you are likely to want to use, and they also have a space for 'other checking point', which you can use when none of the others applies. You should use this only with great care. One use for this is for deaths before 1866, when the age at death is not given in the indexes. Rather than specify an exact age, it is best to give a span of years, as ages on death certificates are often inaccurate. Another use is on a marriage certificate, when you have found a likely entry for the man, but do not know his wife's maiden name; you can use her forename as the checking point. When using any forename as a checking point, remember that they are subject to variations in spelling, and the person concerned may have a middle name of which you were unaware. If you are checking for a father called John, you should add 'with or without any other forenames', which you can abbreviate to (+/-) before and after the name, in case he turns out to be William John or John Edward etc. One of the suggested checking points on death certificate applications is 'Date of birth of deceased (only shown in and after June 1969)'. This is completely pointless, since the date of birth is also shown in the indexes from June 1969. Another one is 'Occupation and (if female) marital condition of deceased'. You may want to check whether a woman's death entry you have found is the right one by specifying that she be widow, spinster or married woman, but occupation is not a good checking point. Quite apart from the fact that someone's occupation might change, the same occupation can be described in different ways; for example 'plumber, painter & glazier' and combinations thereof is a common occupation in the 19th century. It is unreasonable to expect the ONS staff to know that the man you wanted to be a plumber, but who is described as a glazier, is the right one, and they will not issue the certificate. If the certificate does not agree with a checking point, it will be marked 'no' against that point. If the information is not stated it will be marked 'N/S'. Look out for this when you use the father's name as the checking point on a birth, as it may mean your ancestor was illegitimate and 'invented' a father on his or her marriage certificate. If you would like several entries checked for the same checking point, you can complete a separate application for each one, or fill in one form and ask the cashier for a CAS/REF form to list all the others. This cuts down the amount of writing you have to do, and costs less initially (ask for leaflet CAS 62 for more information). You can ask to have all the entries on the list checked, or stop at the first one which agrees. If you use a CAS/REF form, ONS do not guarantee that the certificate (if any) will be ready within the usual four working days, although in most cases it will be. It is therefore not advisable to use this service if time is of the essence. If your certificate is not issued, you will receive a refund, currently of half the cost of the application.

USING THE CENSUS

Now that Census and Civil Registration are in the same building, it is even easier than before to use each of them to help with searches in the other. You can use the census to find out a person's birthplace to help you search for the birth in Civil Registration. You may also be able to find out their age by this means, which is helpful when you have a marriage certificate without exact ages. For a birth before 1881 you should be able to find the person in the index to this Census, the only one which is completely indexed, if you have an idea of the county where they were at that time. If you have several births to choose from in the dozen or so years before 1881, in different places, it is worth looking on the index to the relevant counties to see if you can find a child with a father of the right name, or at least to identify the ones who have fathers with the wrong name, whom you can then cross off your list. Obviously this will work best for births in the late 1870's up to 1881, as the longer the gap between birth and census, the greater the chance that the family has moved to another county, or the father has died, and children in their teens might be living away from their parents. The 1881 census may still be of use if a birth is in the early 1880s and the father has an unusual name. If you find your ancestor in the census with his family, it may give you all sorts of useful clues. For example, if his mother is a widow, this may help to shorten the length of the search for his father's death or will. Other family members may be present, relatives of the mother being particularly useful, as they can tell you her maiden name. This is a great help if you are trying to go straight to the father's marriage because you have been unable to locate a birth certificate. Bear in mind, though, that the information in the census is not always as accurate as it might be. You should always try to locate your ancestors in more than one census whenever possible, in case they show contradictory information about birthplaces, ages, and even relationships, in different years.

The census can also be very helpful for marriages. It is of course a way to establish the ages of the parties, but can tell you so much more. If you find your ancestor as a child in a family group, you may be able to make an educated guess at the approximate date of the parents' marriage from the ages of the children, as well as the parents'. Bearing in mind that census ages are not always accurate, it is a good idea to start your marriage search by working back from the approximate date of birth of the eldest child. This will often help you find a marriage fairly quickly, but you may need to look closely at the family to get the best out of the census. For example, a married couple in their 40's may have children ranging in age from about 19 downwards, but remember that such a couple could have older children who have now left home, so the marriage might be 5 or 6 years before the birth of the 19 year old. This is another good reason for finding the family in as many census years as possible. Another possibility is that your ancestor came from a second marriage. It is not necessarily the case that a man's wife in the census is the mother of all his children. Sometimes this will be easy to spot, such as when the eldest child is 15, and the wife only 25, but in many cases it would be impossible to tell from the census alone. So if you cannot find a marriage before the eldest child's birth, you may have to do it the hard way after all, and work back from the date on the birth certificate you have. On the other hand, you may be lucky and find the married couple aged only about 20 in the census, so you will know that they could not have been married for too long before that. You might even find them before they married, if their names are distinctive enough, which would give you an earliest possible date (June quarter of the census year) in which the marriage could have taken place.

It is worth remembering that both Civil Registration and Census were arranged by Superintendent Registrars' Districts, so that if you are looking for an address taken from a birth or death certificate, this will give you the district and sub-district. This is helpful when there are two or more places in a county with the same name, or one place which is split between two districts. Check to see if towns have street indexes, as knowing the district and sub-district can help identify the correct street if there is more than one with the same name, or a long street which is divided between districts. If a town has no street index, you only need to search one sub-district to find the address, not the whole town. Marriage certificates do not have sub-districts, and in any case, searches based on addresses from them are less likely to be successful as they are often only temporary addresses. Remember, too, that one of the parties, often the man, may well have been resident in another district altogether before the marriage. This is not always obvious from the certificate.

For a fuller account of how to use the Census, see Susan Lumas's *Making Use of the Census.*

USING THE IGI AND OTHER FINDING AIDS (see pages 7-8)

Having all these resources in the same building has made a difference to the way you can conduct your research. Not only can you use the Census to help with Civil Registration searches, and vice versa, but the finding aids and other records on the first floor can also be useful. If you are searching for a birth, the IGI may contain the person's baptism, which in turn might lead to the census; or it might lead to the parents' marriage, and baptisms of brothers and sisters also on the IGI. You should remember that the IGI is only a finding aid, and the original records must always be checked at the first opportunity. In the case of Nonconformist entries before 1837, records of these are in the Family Records Centre (RG 4-8). The lists on the open shelves will give you the full reference. Remember that a baptism was not always shortly after the birth, and in some cases could be years later. While baptisms on the IGI do not always correspond with civil registration of births, marriages are a different matter. Unless the names are very common, a marriage is unmistakable. For the early years of Civil Registration in particular, it is worth looking at the IGI for the county where the marriage is likely to have taken place, and you may find it quite painlessly. You will then have to look at only one (or perhaps two) index books in the ONS Search Room to find the reference to order the certificate. If you have no idea of the location, by using FamilySearch, you can easily search a wider area.

USING PCC WILLS AND DEATH DUTY REGISTERS

When the Civil Registration indexes were at St Catherine's House, it was often a good idea to walk the short distance to Somerset House to search for a will (from 1858 onwards) before embarking on a search for a death, particularly if the search was likely to be long or the name was a common one. While it is still a good idea to check for wills, this now requires planning ahead. However, for the period before 1858, there is now some useful probate material in the same building as the births, marriages and deaths, which is some compensation. Before 1858 wills could be proved in a variety of courts, but increasing numbers of wills and letters of administration from all over England and Wales are found in the PCC towards the end of this period (PROB 11 & PROB 6). Another useful class of records often overlooked is that of the Estate Duty Registers and their indexes. Estate Duty was first imposed in 1796, and applied to only a small proportion of estates until 1815. From that date to 1857, the Indexes (IR 27) provide the nearest there is to a national index of Wills and Letters of Administration. They give the name and abode of the deceased, names of executors, and the court in which the will was proved. This alone can be enough to locate a death certificate (from July 1837), or help in a census search. The registers themselves (IR 26) are even more informative, often containing details not found in the Will, but they are difficult to use. For more information Jane Cox's *Affection Defying the Power of Death: Wills, Probate & Death Duty Records* is strongly recommended.

OTHER RECORDS IN THE FAMILY RECORDS CENTRE

Now that the link with New Register House in Edinburgh is available, researchers with over the Border ancestry will find their task easier, as they can find out whether an event took place in England or Scotland, all in the same room. Although you will still need to apply to New Register House for certificates and extracts from the Census and Old Parochial Registers, at least if you establish that an event took place in Scotland you need not spend any more time searching for it in England. For some other events outside England and Wales there are the Miscellaneous Indexes to Overseas Registrations in the ONS Search Room and Indexes to Miscellaneous Non-statutory Registers on microfilm on the first floor (RG43). There is some overlap between these records, of which more details can be found in the front of the RG43 class list on the open shelves. There are still other records relating to births, marriages and deaths overseas in the Colonial Office and Foreign Office Correspondence records, and Regimental records, all in the PRO at Kew. For the British in India, you should consult the British Library, Oriental & India Office Collections.

USEFUL ADDRESSES

British Library, Oriental & India Office Collections, Orbit House,
   197 Blackfriars Road, London SE1 8NG
Federation of Family History Societies
   Administrator: c/o The Benson Room, Birmingham & Midland Institute,
      Margaret Street, Birmingham B3 3BS
   Publications: 2-4 Killer Street, Ramsbottom, Bury, Lancs BL0 9BZ
London Metropolitan Archives (formerly Greater London Record Office),
   40 Northampton Road, London EC1R 0HB
London Transport Headquarters, 55 Broadway, London SW1H 0BD
New Register House, Edinburgh EH1 3YT
ONS, Postal Applications Section, Smedley Hydro, Trafalgar Road, Birkdale,
   Southport PR8 2HH
Post Office Archives & Records Centre, Freeling House, Mount Pleasant,
   London EC1A 1BB
Principal Registry of the Family Division, Somerset House, Strand,
   London WC2R 1LP
Public Record Office, Kew, Surrey TW9 4DU
Society of Genealogists, 14 Charterhouse Buildings, Goswell Road,
   London EC1M 7BA

BIBLIOGRAPHY

Bevan, Amanda & Duncan, Andrea (eds) *Tracing your Ancestors in
   the Public Record Office,* HMSO 4th edn. 1990
Cox, Jane, *An Introduction to Affection Defying the Power of Death:
   Wills, Probate & Death Duty Records,* FFHS 1993
Lumas, Susan, *Making Use of the Census,* PRO 1992
Nissel, Muriel, *People Count,* HMSO 1987
Pelling, George, *Beginning Your Family History,* FFHS 6th edn. 1995
Rogers, Colin, *Family Tree Detective,* Manchester University Press 1985
Saul, Pauline, *The Family Historian's Enquire Within,* FFHS 5th edn. 1995
Wiggins, R., *St Catherine's House Districts*
Wood, Tom, *An Introduction to Civil Registration,* FFHS 1994
Wood, Tom, *Basic Facts About Using Record Offices for Family
   Historians,* FFHS 1996
District Register Offices in England & Wales, East Yorkshire FHS 1997
Registration Districts in England & Wales 1837-1851, and 1852-1946,
   (maps), Institute of Heraldic & Genealogical Studies (Northgate,
   Caterbury, Kent CT1 1BA)